WISEUP Adventure Series

Chris & Key 6

Christian Wise Smith

Illustrated by Willie Williams Jr. & Destiny Woodard

Library of Congress Control Number: 2021900446

ISBN 978-1-7364556-0-9 (paperback)

ISBN 978-1-7364556-2-3 (hardcover)

For my Wife & Best Friend Keonda;
my kids, Christian II, Adlai, Luca, and Kayden;
and for all of the future voters and leaders who
will make our world even better one day.

WISEUP!

"Time for breakfast, Chris and Key!
Today is a very special day!"

"Oh, really, Grandpa Wise?
What's happening today?"

"We get to use our Superpower!

It's Election Day!"

"We have a superpower, Grandpa Wise?
How do we use it?" asked Key.

"It's the right to vote,
Sweet Potato.

We get to pick the leaders for our
city, state, and country!"

BALLOT
BOX

"Does everyone have this superpower,
Grandpa Wise?" asked Chris.

"We all do now, Champ, but it was not
always like this.

We did not have the right to vote
because of the color of our skin.

Women could not vote either.
The superpower was only for white men.

10

WE MARCH FOR
JOBS FOR ALL NOW!
WE DEMAND VOTING RIGHTS NOW!
GIVE US THE VOTE!
VOTE
VOTES FOR WOMEN

12

Dr. Martin Luther King, Jr., John Lewis, Fannie Lou Hamer, and others worked really hard to get everyone this superpower," said Grandpa Wise.

"People protested.
People marched in the streets.
Some people even lost their lives."

"So, now that everyone has this superpower, who are the leaders that we pick,
Grandpa Wise?" asked Key.

"Well, the legislative, executive, and judicial branches make up our government tree.

They are men and women like the president, city council members, and judges who represent what's best for you and me."

14

15

16

"What do they do for us, Grandpa Wise?"
Chris asked without pause.

"Well, Champ,
city council members make laws.
The president enforces laws.
And judges explain laws."

"How do we vote?" asked Key.

"We go to our local voting poll location to fill out an election ballot. We put a check mark next to the name that we want to represent us, you see."

VOTE
VOTE
VOTE
VOTE

STADIUM
BASKETBALL
"VOTE HERE"

"Do we get to vote for anything else,
Grandpa Wise?" asked Chris.

"We also get to vote to change laws and
policies. They are called ballot measures.

Time to hop in the car, Chris and Key.
To the basketball arena we go!

We're going to use our
SUPERPOWER,
the power to vote!"

Grandpa Wise filled out his ballot with
Chris and Key by his side.

They all got an "I Voted" sticker that
they wore with great pride!

VIP
I VOTED
I VOTED
I VOTED
23

NOW LET'S HAVE SOME FUN!

IT'S YOUR TURN TO VOTE!

Complete a Voter Registration Card and cast your ballot to vote for your favorite color!

Voter Registration Card
NAME
BIRTHDAY
AGE
TEACHER
SCHOOL
SIGNATURE

VOTE
FAVORITE COLOR
RED
BLUE
YELLOW
PURPLE
GREEN
ORANGE

27

WHAT SUPERPOWER DID CHRIS & KEY DISCOVER?

WHO HELPED GET EVERYONE THE RIGHT TO VOTE?

1

____

2

____

3

____

NAME THE THREE BRANCHES OF GOVERNMENT

1

____

2

____

3

____

WISEUP Adventure Series
Chris & Key Go Vote!
CONGRATULATIONS
You learned how to vote by completing the
first book in the WISEUP Adventure Series!
SIGNATURE
DATE

WISEUP

Made in United States
Orlando, FL
29 March 2022

16274124R00020